GOING THE DISTANCE WITH GOD

BY LORI SALIERNO
With Esther Bailey

Going the Distance with God

By Lori Salierno
With Esther Bailey

Designed by Paul Johnson
Edited by Robin K. Fogle

ISBN: 0-87162-688-8
D7554
Printed in Mexico

Copyright © 1995 Warner Press, Inc.
All rights reserved.

Acknowledgements

The excerpts featured in this book are taken from *Designed for Excellence*, by Lori Salierno with Esther Bailey, © 1995 Warner Press, Inc.

Cover Photo by West Stock, Inc./Brian Drake.

All scripture quotations are taken from the New Revised Standard Version of the Bible, © 1989, Division of Christian Education of the National Council of Churches of Christ in the United States of America. Used by permission. All rights reserved.

INTRODUCTION

Will you go the distance with God? If you have ever felt like giving up, lift your eyes to heaven now and say, "God, I'll never quit on you!" Keep your love affair with God fresh through daily renewal. Focus on Jesus. When people fail you, fix your eyes on Jesus. Determine within yourself that no matter what happens, you're going to make it through. With Jesus on your side, you can do it!

Lori Salierno

Does your spirit demand a signature of excellence on everything you do? Is your work a praise offering to God? You may work on something simple today, but if you do your best, tomorrow may bring success beyond your highest expectations. The master of the faithful servant said, "You have been trustworthy in a few things, I will put you in charge of many things; enter into the joy of your master" (Matthew 25:21).

Many people believe that the Christian life is dull. Some Christians even believe they are missing out on the fun because they serve the Lord. That idea comes from Satan. God doesn't want us to miss out on anything good in life. God's salvation offers us a joyful life.

If you're not enjoying school or work, maybe you need to change your attitude. Work, either at school or on the job, is not something we do just to get by. Work is an opportunity, a privilege, given to us by God. Work provides us with the opportunity to develop virtue, or moral excellence. Virtue, in turn, helps create habits that strengthen character.

God's standard of living is higher than the standard the world sets. God's standard, clearly stated in the Bible as God's will, is a universal principle that applies to all people no matter where they live or what their culture is like. God says to Christians, I want to lift you high above mediocrity. I want to exhibit you as an example of my high quality of creativity. If you will pay the price to govern your life by God's standards, you can be that example.

As a young man, D. L. Moody sat in church and heard the preacher say, "The world has yet to see the person who has surrendered to Jesus Christ one hundred percent." In the moment that D. L. Moody heard that statement, he said in his heart, "Lord, I will be that person." Thousands of people came to know Jesus through his ministry because he surrendered himself completely to the Lord.

When we look at our work and see nothing but rubbish, we must refocus our eyes on God. No honorable work is too lowly, no task is too insignificant to merit our signature of excellence. A job well done becomes a praise offering to God.

God's not calling you to bring people to a decision about their salvation. Only God can do that. Our responsibility is simply to share the gospel and show people how to live the Christian life. God will do the rest.

New Christians may wonder what kind of guarantee God gives them. Even mature Christians may ask what kind of warranty goes along with their Christian service. The answer?

None! Absolutely none!

God does not guarantee success just because you are a Christian.

When Jesus was born, God threw the grandest party of all time. What host or hostess could match the appearance of an angelic chorus singing about the good news of great joy? (Luke 2:10). The reason for the party was the fulfillment of the promise of forgiveness. We who have been set free from sin's bondage through the blood of Jesus have just begun to live life to the fullest.

God, thank You for sending Your Son as a sacrifice for my sins. Thank You for forgiving my sins. I accept with gratitude Your forgiveness and Your gift of eternal life. You know how easy it is to allow wrong attitudes, selfish interests, and human weakness to hinder my relationship with You. I offer myself in total surrender to You. Lord, surround me with Your love and pour out Your Spirit on me in a fresh, new way. Give me power to begin a dynamic, victorious walk with You. I pray in Jesus' name. Amen.

How much is it worth to you to be in the center of God's will? Would you exchange the joy and peace that accompany obedience for any amount of money? You can be rich spiritually even if you are poor in the wealth of the world.

Confession is often painful but necessary to bring about a sense of oneness between God and you. Not only does confession involve asking forgiveness for failures that you recognize, it also consists of allowing God to reveal to you anything else in your life that is wrong. With a clean slate between you and God, you're ready to move ahead in your worship experience.

God designed the church so that the members are dependent upon God and upon one another. We need God and God needs us. Without us, God may not choose to act. Without God, we cannot hope to accomplish anything that will last. Christian ministry is done through human hands but not by human hands. It requires an alliance between the divine and the human. "Take courage, all you people of the land, says the Lord; work, for I am with you, says the Lord of hosts" (Haggai 2:4).

When Christians fall on their knees, or even pray in their hearts, they are tapping power, love, and all that God is in such a way that God becomes a real part of their lives. Prayer totally transforms us physically, emotionally, and spiritually in such a way that we influence everyone around us. With that kind of motivation to pray, do we need to be entertained? Does God need to tickle our fancy before we'll pray?

God designed the plan of salvation, Jesus paid the price with His death, and the Holy Spirit invites us to accept Jesus as Saviour. We need only pray a simple but sincere prayer such as, "Lord Jesus, I need You. I believe You are the Son of God and I accept You as my Saviour. Forgive my sins and come into my life. Amen."

Don't give God your leftover time. Give God your prime time when you're at your best. If you're most alert in the morning, give God time in the morning. If you're a night person, give God time in the evening. If you really get going about noon, give God your lunch break. Allow God to break in on your thoughts throughout the day, but set aside some specific time for just the two of you to be together.

The name of Jesus has greater power than anything else on earth. When we pray in the name of Jesus, we connect with His power. When we speak in His name, we connect with His power. We can impact both the unseen and the physical world through the power in Jesus' name.

If you seek to be God's example of excellence, you must govern your life with biblical standards and develop Christian convictions that lead you to become all that God designed you to be.

God, thank You for creating me, redeeming me, and giving me Your Word to help me become the person You designed me to be. Thank You for the guidance I receive through prayer, circumstances, and through the counsel of other Christians. Help me remain submissive to Your will and to practice what is right. Help me place my trust in You and not lean on my own understanding.

In the precious name of Jesus, I pray. Amen.

To get the most from your work, ignore your critics, focus on God, fight failure, and never complain. Whether you empty trash or design computers, whether you're a blue-collar worker or a white-collar worker, consider your work as a gift from God and use it to develop virtue—a character trait that brands you as a Christian.

We renew our commitments to God the same way we were born again. John instructed those who had lost their first love to repent and do the works they did at first (Revelation 2:5). Admit your need to be restored to spiritual wholeness. Ask God to forgive you for a lukewarm attempt to live the Christian life. Confess any actions or attitudes that are wrong. Ask God to send the Holy Spirit in a fresh, new way. Open your heart to God's Spirit and seek to live daily in the Spirit.

Whether you're facing a major

crisis or a minor frustration,

God will walk through it with you.

Pull good memories from the past,

separate the goodness of God

from the injustices of life,

hang on to your integrity,

glorify God,

and keep your hope alive.

What power we have in the name of Jesus! Even the sound of his name causes Satan to tremble. When we pray in the name of Jesus, we not only move God, we defeat the enemy as well. "The Son of God was revealed for this purpose, to destroy the works of the devil" (1 John 3:8). When Jesus comes on the scene, Satan must flee.

As you work toward making your goal, there will be times when you feel like throwing up your hands and saying, "I can't do it!" Actually, that's a positive sign because it forces you to recognize your human limitations. Tell God you're stuck and you need help. Scripture promises "To him who by the power at work within us is able to accomplish abundantly far more than all we can ask or imagine, to him be glory in the church" (Ephesians 3:20, 21). Praise God, your vision is a mighty force that can be energized through the power of Jesus Christ working within you!

The key to successful living is endurance. You need endurance in school, on the job, and in your Christian life—particularly in your Christian life. Jesus said, "The one who endures to the end will be saved" (Matthew 10:22). When you're humiliated, don't give up. If someone ignores you at church, don't quit. If you feel God has deserted you, remember the Lord's promise to be ever present with you. If you disappoint yourself and God, do not despair. Keep trying until you turn your failure into success.

Even as you stand in darkness, full of confusion and fear, God can work in and through you. No life need be lived in vain. You may never reach your desired goal or even the goal you think God has set. But how you handle your desert experiences is important to God because God is developing your spirituality. The end result of the process is what matters.

Do you know at what point your frustrating, irritating, disappointing work will turn into a playday? When you overcome poor attitudes and fear of failure. And the harder you work to win, the greater will be your pleasure when you achieve success.

How can we abide in Christ?

The only way we can abide in Christ,

the only way we can bear fruit,

the only way we can know God

intimately is through prayer.

We cannot move toward

spiritual maturity,

much less excellence,

without prayer.

Almighty God, I speak Your name in awe and reverence because of who You are. You are Creator, Redeemer, Friend, the Source of all life. I feel insignificant in Your presence, Lord, especially as I recognize my failures. Forgive me for the times I have allowed anything but You to take first place in my life. Help me fulfill my destiny by abiding in You. Thank You for Your love and for the privilege of knowing You. In Jesus' name I pray. Amen.

Never give up hope! You can endure a terrible today if you expect a better tomorrow. Although your circumstances may seem hopeless, God may lift your burden at a moment's notice. On the other hand, you may be locked into a situation for life. In those cases we hinge hope on heaven. "This slight momentary affliction is preparing us for an eternal weight of glory beyond all measure" (2 Corinthians 4:17).

When you are trying to do your best for God, either inside or outside the church, you'll meet with opposition. A guy in the shipping department of a small company was hustling to get out tools that customers wanted. "What are you trying to do—cheat us out of our overtime?" a co-worker said. Don't allow anyone to rob you of the joy of work through ridicule.

Our joy pleases God.... Our joy inspires other believers (those who are being saved) and is attractive to the unchurched (those who are perishing). As we joyfully celebrate our victory in Jesus, we encourage other Christians who may be going through a difficult time. Simply by revealing the joy of the Lord, we cause the ungodly to recognize there is value in serving God.

Are you at a crossroads in your life? Do you have an important decision to make? Are you anxious about an uncertain future? With the Word of God inscribed in your heart and a prayer on your lips, look for God's harbor lights and go forth to face the unknown with confidence.

Halfway through high school or college the tough times ahead may drain you of enthusiasm. Perhaps your job is about to do you in. Call time out. Seek counsel from someone who has made it through school or someone who understands your job—perhaps your teacher or boss. Draw from the wisdom and experience of someone who knows what you are going through. As you pray, allow God to refresh your spirit, and nothing can keep you down.

God is fair, but life is not always fair. If we confuse God's justice with physical life, we set ourselves up for disappointment. We run the risk of understanding faith as a bargaining tool. "God, I'll serve you as long as you come through for me." A faith based upon the necessity of social justice will crumble when the road gets rough. Christian faith centers upon a personal relationship with God, through Christ, rather than upon life's circumstances.

The very nature of riches fosters a fake sense of security. While knowing where the next meal will come from is comforting, the feeling that wealth can supply every need is deceptive and blasphemous. Trusting in riches eliminates dependence upon God.

It takes discipline to program your mind with joy.

Someone may spread a vicious rumor about you. A friendship may turn sour. You may not be able to get a job, or you may not have the money to go to college. Paul wrote, "In any and all circumstances I have learned the secret of being well-fed and of going hungry, of having plenty and of being in need" (Philippians 4:12). You may hurt inside, but you can still have the kind of joy that's anchored in God's love.

Jesus, You are my example as I learn to deal with suffering in this world. No matter what happens, I will never be called upon to suffer as You suffered. I am grateful You understand what it's like to be human and feel weak and oppressed. Thank You for offering to help carry heavy burdens. Help me give You my sorrows and accept Your healing touch. In Your precious name I pray. Amen.

You don't have to be an uptight, grim-faced Christian who hates yourself!... Be yourself! As long as you reflect God's glory, you have freedom. If you're the quiet, reserved, intellectual type, don't try to bounce off the walls.... Let God use your personality as it is. You are unique. If some people don't like the way you are, that's okay. Not everyone can like you, but never allow anyone to make you feel you are less worthy than somebody else.

If you're living by all the truth revealed to you through Scripture, you can count on God to guide you in the optional area. When you put together God's Word with prayer as a basis for your spiritual life, you are in powerful form! You are moving toward excellence in a dynamic fashion.

Do you realize we can fulfill our destinies only through prayer? Prayer is our lifeline. God created us in order to have fellowship with us. How can we maintain a casual attitude toward prayer when we are so important to God?

God, I lift my heart in everlasting

praise to You because You have

redeemed me through the blood of Jesus.

Thank You for your promise to take me

through to the end. Help me feel

Your presence and know You are as

close to me as my own breath.

Draw me back to You if I should stray.

In Jesus' holy name I pray. Amen.

Improving your appearance won't make God love you more, but it may make you feel better about yourself. A more positive self-image will contribute to your overall well-being. Once you do all you can to correct any physical flaws, accept your appearance as a gift from God. If you are not self-conscious about your imperfections, others will notice them less.

As students or workers, Christians should be the best workers on the job. We should be the ones who come back from lunch early. We should be the ones who support our employers and treat our co-workers with respect. We represent God to the world, and the signature we place on everything we do should match our profession of Christianity.

As a Christian, you will have trouble maintaining your self-esteem unless you keep your spiritual experience up to date. Actually, your only claim to excellence comes through the Lord. "Let the one who boasts, boast in the Lord" (2 Corinthians 10:17). It is not what you do that deserves acclaim but what God does through you.

A vision represents something that hasn't yet happened. It's something you foresee in the future as taking place for God. In ministry, your vision becomes your goal and you pursue it with passion. Don't be afraid to dream big. The bigger your dream, the greater your potential to make a worthwhile contribution to God.

You were not a mistake when you were created, but God will continue to fashion you according to your destiny if you will cooperate. With God's refiner's wheel and furnace, the rough edges of your life will be smoothed away and your personality will reflect beauty from within. As you yield to the Holy Spirit's control, God's image will be yours. It will show in your life and you can feel good about yourself.

God, thank You for creating me in Your image. Thank You for loving me the way I am. Help me to love and accept myself as You do. Help me to accept myself the way You created me. Help me to enjoy being the person You created me to be. May I make the most of the personality, talents, and gifts You have given me. In the name of Jesus I pray. Amen.

Do you realize that praise is the one thing we do for God that God cannot do alone? What an incredible thought! Praise is the one gift we can give to the One who has given so much to us. Communion with God is a privilege.

You can know the mind of God (1 Corinthians 2:16)! Your heart, your will, can be in such complete harmony with God's will that they are one. We don't have to wonder if God's gonna go "poof" and disappear. God doesn't say, "See, I'm over here, but you guys are over there," in some sort of hide and seek game. God wants us to know His will.

A sixteenth-century monk named Brother Lawrence spent his entire life in the kitchen of the monastery washing dishes. Brother Lawrence might not have had menial labor in mind when he took his vows to become a monk, but he prayed as he washed dishes, "Lord, be glorified in these clean dishes." He turned the kitchen into a sanctuary of praise, and people who worked with him sensed God's presence in the kitchen.

If you want to go the distance with God, you must move ahead one step at a time. You can't sit around waiting for spiritual maturity to happen because it will not happen without effort on your part. You must progress day by day. As you absorb more of God's Word into your heart and mind, as you get to know God better through prayer, as you share God's love with others, you grow stronger for the journey.

The sickness of sin calls for an old-fashioned dose of repentance. "Repent therefore, and turn to God so that your sins may be wiped out" (Acts 3:19). Repentance is ongoing and involves change. It includes a turning away from anything that stands between God and us. It is through this change, this renewing of our minds that stems from repentance, that we become new creatures in Christ. The nature of change will vary according to the circumstances and the personalities of all individuals.

Joy is an attitude rather than a feeling. Whether we have a personality that bubbles over or bombs out, we can choose to base our attitudes on the victory we share in Christ. We can develop an attitude of joy.

An exercise in thanksgiving

benefits us at the same time

it pleases God. When we tell

God how grateful we are,

God spills the praise back

on us and our joy is full.

It is impossible to be miserable

and full of thanksgiving

at the same time.

What do we get from church that we need? As we participate in worship with other Christians, we are inspired. As we sing praises together and unite our hearts in prayer, we are strengthened. As we hear God's Word preached, we hide it in our hearts to keep us from sin. Powerful messages and good illustrations help us better apply God's Word to our lives.

Will you lift your heart in praise to God who sent Jesus to bring abundant life to us? Will you recognize that life can beat you up but it can't beat you down if the joy of the Lord is your strength? If life has grown stale for you, God is ready to restore your joy. You can then join the royal party prepared for you by the King of kings.